A CONVENIENT BEGINNERS GUIDE TO ESSENTIAL OILS AND AROMATHERAPY

NATURAL ESSENTIAL OIL RECIPES for HEALTH AND WELL-BEING

WILLIAM MOORE

Readers acknowledge that the author is not engaging in the rendering of legal, financial, medical or professional advice. The content within this book has been derived from various sources.

By reading this document, the reader agrees that under no circumstances is the author responsible for any losses, direct or indirect, which are incurred as a result of the use of the information contained within this document, including, but not limited to, — errors, omissions, or inaccuracies.

ISBN: 9798686124202

Table of Contents

Introduction

From the author

In this book, you will learn the most important information and necessary knowledge about essential oils.

This book tells you everything you need to know about essential oils and their uses. The mystery of choice and a wide range of the use of essential oils is revealed, as well as the criteria needed to determine the quality of an essential oil.

The book is presented in a simple and understandable language, filled with specific data, as a result, all the content reflects the very essence of this book - namely, what essential oils are needed for and how everyone can use this natural gift with maximum benefit for themselves in their lives.

This book immerses the reader into the fascinating world of essential oils and gives a new useful knowledge of nature.

Enjoy your read!

Essential oils- sources

The use of essential oils in aromatherapy and skincare has been known since ancient times. Evidence of the use of essential oils was found during the time of the Egyptian pharaohs, the ancient Greeks, and the Romans. Even then, essential oils were used for weight loss and were also widely used. The most beautiful women of that time could not do without their essential hair and essential facial oils.

In ancient times, the healing power of aromas and plants was widely known and with the help of them, the body and soul were often treated.

In the Old Testament, incense such as sandal and myrrh are mentioned.

Ancient Egyptians used essential oils extensively for medical and cosmetic purposes. In ancient Egypt, balms made from myrrh, juniper, and incense tree were used for religious rites.

In ancient Greece, Hippocrates described the properties of more than 200 herbs that he actively used for treatment. Hippocrates, Avicenna, and Galen described in their writings the entire spectrum of the use of incense and argued that with the help of essential oils any disease could be defeated. The famous scientist and physician Avicenna were the first to receive oil from rose petals, through steam distillation.

It is safe to state that oils have always been considered a noble mean of healing. Today there are many varieties. The range of their applications is also relatively wide.

Essential oils are a potent substance. It is necessary to clearly observe dosages and recommendations. Pregnant women and people with allergies need to be especially careful.

If you choose essential oils for weight loss, hair, for the skin and face, then their effect will improve not only the appearance but also health, sexual function, and the state of the nervous system. That is why the use of essential oils and aromatherapy with essential oils is often called aroma magic.

Essential oils are an excellent addition to the care of your skin, hair, and can also be useful for medical purposes. They can also be used for aromatherapy, as an addition to massage oils and to create a relaxing atmosphere.

Essential oils for hair and the skin are extracted from the different parts of a plant, and these processes are unusually complex. It is important to preserve all the beneficial properties of plants, so that their healing power helps maintain health and beauty.

Can essential hair oils, skin oils, and weight loss oils be as effective as salon beauty treatments? In many cases, they can. For this, almost the entire range of essential oils are used as active components in the creation of professional cosmetics.

Chapter 1: Everything you need to know about essential oils

1. What is Essential Oil?

Essential oil is an aromatic-concentrated, volatile liquid composition, which is produced by plants and is the source of their aroma.

Essential oils are formed in all parts of the plant - roots, stems, leaves and flowers. For example, rose, jasmine, ylang-ylang, lavender, tuberose - in flowers. In mint, geranium, rosemary, eucalyptus - in the stem and leaves. Essential oils are contained in seeds of carrots, anise, cardamom, cumin, fennel, dill. Oils can even be found in plant roots. For example - air, iris, vetiver, ginger.

In essential oils there are chemical compounds that have therapeutic properties.

The chemical composition is quite complex, it has many interconnected substances, such as esters, terpenes, ketones, lactones, alcohols, aldehydes, aromatic components, and others.

Essential oils are extracted from different parts of plants in several ways:

- Distillation with steam or vacuum (distillation).
- Maceration - extract from plants using vegetable oils with a neutral odor. The fatty component is then removed by alcohols. The same principle is based on the extraction process using non-polar solvents.
- Cold pressing. It is used to extract valuable components from the peel of fruits.
- Enfleurage- absorption by fats. The method is applicable to particularly rare plants.

Oils are obtained from pleasantly smelling flowers, herbs, shrubs, or trees, which in turn attract pollinator insects. Or vice versa, of those plant species that scare off insect pests. In this regard, there is a huge variety of oils, differing from each other in their aroma, color, and method of production. At the same time, the quality of essential oils may also vary, such factors as variety and type of plant, growing conditions, age of the plant, time of collection of natural material, and others affect this condition.

Essential oils differ from conventional base oils in that they have the property of rapidly volatilizing, that is, they instantly evaporate at room temperature, filling the air with a characteristic aroma. This is how they got their name, because of the high evaporation rate, they look like ethers. These oils are perfectly soluble in alcohol, ether, fatty oils or waxes, but are not soluble in water.

2. Essential oil groups

Each essential oil is unique and has its own unique properties.

There is no definite classification of essential oils, however, manufacturers conditionally distinguish two main features, from which they are divided into groups:

- Parts of the plant; In relation to the method of their production, the main raw materials are plants, or rather parts of them. If we note that several different essential oils can be obtained from one botanical species, then the number of its species increases significantly.

- By the influence on the human body: The effect of essential oils on the human body or a certain organ, implies a result of a chemical reaction that occurs through inhalation. Thus, essential oil, consisting of hundreds of different components, entering the human blood, begins to interact with hormones and enzymes. As a result, a person can experience different sensations in the form of relaxation or arousal, calmness or a tide of energy.

3. Types of essential oils by plants

Types of essential oils by plants:

3.1. Flower

These are oils extracted from the flower or bud of the plant. These include rose oils, jasmine, chamomile, ylang-ylang, neroli, lavender, lotus, geranium, and others. These species have a persistent, sweet aroma. They are considered to be a group of anti-stress oils.

Flower oils have found their widespread use in the field of perfumery, for the manufacture of cosmetics, in skin and hair care products.

Useful qualities of flower oils:

- ✓ Relaxing, pacifying effect (except jasmine oil - it has a tonic effect), sleep normalization;
- ✓ Getting rid of migraine and headache;
- ✓ Beneficial effects on the human nervous system, stress relief, harmonization of the internal state;

- ✓ The rejuvenating effect achieved by the active effect of oils on skin cells. Often added to masks and creams;
- ✓ Active elimination of toxins;
- ✓ Immunostimulatory properties;
- ✓ Excellent hair care product. Oils will help to get rid of split ends, strengthen hair and restore roots.

3.2. Grassy

These are oils obtained directly from the stems of plants. These include sage oils, mint, rosemary, anise, basil, thyme, laurel, eucalyptus herbs, tea tree, and others.

Such essential oils have a tonic effect, and eliminate accumulated fatigue and stress.

They are actively used in medicine due to their useful indicators.

Useful qualities of herbal oils:

- ✓ Used as antiseptic drugs,
- ✓ Used for medical care, compression,
- ✓ Have anti-inflammatory qualities,
- ✓ Facilitate rapid tightening of wounds, cuts,
- ✓ Strengthen the immune system,
- ✓ Help eliminate respiratory tract infections, useful for inhalation.

3.3. Sheet

These are oils extracted from the leaves of plants and trees. These include coniferous essential oils. These are eucalyptus oils, spruce, fir, mint, pine, cypress, and others.

These are refreshing oils and they feature a rich aroma that may not appeal to everyone. But at the same time, they are effective in colds.

Useful qualities of refreshing oils:

- ✓ Work as antiseptics,
- ✓ Freshen the air thanks to the persistent aroma. Often used as an analog of air fresheners,
- ✓ The bactericidal properties of oils contribute to the removal of inflammation, the cure of colds,
- ✓ Stimulate the proper functioning of the gastrointestinal tract.

3.4. Wood

Oils derived from wood, bark, or tree resin. These include sandal, cedar, patchouli, camphor, benzoin, incense, and other wood oils. They have a gravitational and dense smell.

Oils of this group help relax after stress.

Useful qualities of wood oils:

✓ Improvement of blood circulation, restoration of normal pulse operation;
✓ Lower blood pressure, have a soothing and relaxing effect;
✓ Wound healing due to the presence of ketones in the oil. The ketone in its pure form is camphor oil;
✓ A calming action;
✓ Are a great moisturizer for dry skin.

3.5. Fruit

These are oils from the fruits of trees or shrubs. These include oils of orange, lemon, grapefruit, bergamot, tangerine, juniper, pepper, melisa and others. Among the variety of fruit essential oils, the citrus group occupies an honorable place.

 Citrus essential oils are used in perfumery and cosmetology, and they are also immune activators. Therefore, they are often recommended for the prevention and treatment of colds. It is worth noting that a feature of the flavors of this group is their inexpensive cost, since the raw materials for the production of such oils are relatively easy to obtain.

Useful qualities of citrus oils:

- ✓ Prevention of colds, assistance in the fight against viral diseases, restoration of immunity;
- ✓ An invigorating, activating action that tones a person, they are often used by drivers on long-distance routes, so they do not fall asleep while driving;

- ✓ Improving brain activity;
- ✓ Stabilizing the body's circulatory system;
- ✓ Fat cleavage, whereby it is actively used in anti-cellulite procedures;
- ✓ Cleansing the body of harmful toxins;
- ✓ Melisa oil, lemon have anti-inflammatory qualities;
- ✓ Increased mood.

Important! Citrus oils are not recommended for use before bedtime, since their action is aimed at boosting activity during the day.

3.6. Spicy oils

Prepared from cinnamon, ginger, nutmeg, pepper, cloves, cardamom. They have a bright and sharp aroma.

Useful qualities of spicy oils:

✓ An exciting effect on the nervous system of the body,
✓ Used to activate brain function,
✓ Lifting mood withdrawn from a depressive state,
✓ Produce a warming effect,
✓ Have protective properties,
✓ Used in the treatment of joints.

3.7. Seed

Oils obtained directly from seeds of plants or vegetables.

 These include carrot oils, dill, sesame and others. This group of essential oils is quite specific, so they are used mainly in the culinary arts.

Useful qualities of seed oils:

- ✓ Regenerating
- ✓ Painkillers
- ✓ Anti-inflammatory
- ✓ Soothing
- ✓ Sedative

3.8. Root

Oils extracted from plant roots. Prominent representatives of this group are turmeric and ginger oils.

Useful qualities of root oils:

✓ high anti-inflammatory properties;
✓ strengthening and antiviral properties so will be effective for colds;
✓ strong tonic property.

4. Types of essential oils by the effect on the human body

4.1. Cleansing
Orange, geranium, lavender, orange, lemon, rosemary, tuberose, sage, rose.

4.2. Exciting
Bergamot, bigardia, geranium, jasmine, ylang-ylang, cardamom, mandarin, rose, sandal.

4.3. Toning
Basil, bay, cloves, ginger, cinnamon, lemon, mint, melissa, nutmeg, palmarosa, fir, rosemary, citronella, thyme, sage.

4.4. Weakening
Valeriana, shower, jasmine, lavender, incense, myrrh, juniper, sandal, chamomile.

4.5. Harmonizing
Orange, geranium, ash, jasmine, mandarin, mimosa, majorana, rose, sandal, most extracts from flowers.

4.6. Strengthening
Basil, verbena, vetiver, cedar, cajeput, lemon, lavender, mint, melissa, rosemary, nutmeg.

4.7. Refreshing

Orange, immortal, lemon, lavender, mint, fir, mandarin.

4.8. Stimulating

Immortal, verbena, cloves, coriander, lemon, lavender, nutmeg, juniper, mint, rosemary, black pepper, eucalyptus, hyssop, pine, fir, lemon.

4.9. Calming

Bigardia, vanilla, geranium, jasmine, melissa, chamomile, dill, mint, incense.

4.10. Antistress

Most extracts from flowers.

5. Properties of essential oils

Essential oils and their properties should be known and understood by everyone. The following describes all the beneficial properties of essential oils that are available today. By studying essential oils, their properties and their use, it is possible to use them with benefit at home.

It is useful to add a few drops of oil matching your skin type to your face mask. Thus, its efficiency is greatly improved. In addition, all essential oils, in addition to the therapeutic effect that they have on the skin, also affect the state of mind. Therefore, by using them, you can take care of your beauty needs, as well as your mood. If desired, you can also add a couple of drops of essential oil to your regular face and body cream.

The properties depend on the type of plant, the part used, the growing conditions, as well as the method of their production. At the same time, their quality, composition and aroma of oil will ultimately be different.

Their properties directly depend on chemical composition. Most essential oils have similar properties, but each has its own exceptional qualities:

5.1. Antibacterial

This property is inherent in most essential oils. Oils rich in phenols and aldehydes have such properties. By having this property, essential oils are able to affect various types of bacteria and fungi. Such oils include thyme oils, cloves, fragrances, anise, basil, bergamot, lemon, grapefruit, juniper and lemongrass.

5.2. Anti-inflammatory and anti-infectious

These are properties of essential oils rich in sesquiterpenes. These properties are also characteristic of many types of essential oils. Due to these properties, essential oils are able to exert early regeneration to the skin during injuries and reduce the permeability of vessels. Bright representatives are the oils of chamomile, millennium, bergamot, ylang-ylang, lavender, juniper and tea tree.

5.3. Antiseptic

This property is characteristic of many types of essential oils. It helps fight bacterial and viral infections effectively. These are oils rich in alcohol (monoterpenes). They are oils of mayorana, tea tree, neroli, anise, orange, bergamot, cloves, lavender, juniper, mint, petitgrain, patchouli and eucalyptus.

5.4. Anesthetic

This property helps to eliminate various problems associated with headaches, insomnia, or nervous exhaustion. Peppermint oils, lavender, blue spruce, immortal, jasmine, balsamic fir have such properties.

5.5. Expectorant

This property helps to facilitate sputum release by exerting a reflex effect on the bronchial mucosa. These are oils rich in oxides. These include oils of eucalyptus, anise, turpentine and cajeput.

5.6. Antioxidant

This property contributes to slowing down the signs of aging, improving blood circulation and lymph flow and stimulating cellular respiration. These include oils of dahlia, millennial, juniper and fir.

5.7. Slowing down the aging process

These are oils containing unique phytohormones, which are similar in structure to human ones. Among them are sandal oils, jasmine, rose, myrrh, patchouli and neroli.

5.8. Promoting Weight Loss

These oils have regulating and burning properties. The effect of them will be noticeable if you use courses locally, arranging a massage session, taking a bath, or wrapping problem areas. These include oils of lemon, grapefruit, cinnamon, bergamot, tea tree and muscat.

5.9. Regulating Sleep

These are oils with warming and calming properties. These oils contain esters and aliphatic aldehydes. These include oils of melissa, incense, rose, mint, cypress, bergamot, sage, sandal, juniper, lavender and ylang-ylang.

5.10. Eliminating insects

These are oils or mixtures that have a specific aroma that mosquitoes or certain insects do not like. The best species for eliminating annoying pests are lavender, rosemary, eucalyptus, mint, vanilla, cloves and geranium.

6. The benefits of essential oils to the body

Essential oils have beneficial effects on a person's mental and physical health. They normalize the work of the nervous and endocrine systems and restore the aquatic balance. In addition, oils remove toxins from the body, which positively affects the skin and hair.

All kinds of essential oils benefit the human immune system.
The benefits of essential oils lies in the properties of their constituents:

✓ Ketones promote wound healing. The pure ketone is camphor. A large number of ketones have been found in the chemical composition of sage, rosemary, hyssop, and eucalyptus.

✓ Ethers work as antiseptics, antispasmodics, and diuretics. They contain cloves, basil, parsley, anise and tarragon.

✓ Aldehydes have anti-inflammatory, soothing, and antiviral properties. The benefits of aldehydes are in melissa, lemon and citronella.

✓ Sesquiterpenes have high immunostimulatory properties. They are useful sedative and bactericidal effects. A large number of sesquiterpenes were found in chamomile, velvet and immortelle.

✓ Phenols have bactericidal and warming properties. They are rich in cinnamon and cloves.

✓ Terpenes burn fats and are useful as antiviruses. These oils are orange, lemon, pine and nutmeg.

✓ Alcohols benefit from their antiseptic and antiprotective properties. Many alcohols contain myrtle, patchouli, sandal, ginger and tea tree.

✓ Active molecules of ether vapors neutralize bacteria and viruses contained in air. They work as disinfectors of air masses.

✓ When exposed to essential oils, active leukocyte production is launched in the human body. Leukocytes are the basis of the work of immunity.

7. Essential oils and their effects

Essential oils primarily affect the psyche and then the internal organs of a person.

Due to their structure, essential oil molecules easily penetrate into our body through the sense of smell or skin. Then a signal is sent to our brain, and through the nervous system, which is then transmitted to the internal organs.

Smells trigger a whole reaction inside our bodies. Remember how your body responds instantly to some smells, causing pleasant memories or hostility. Some flavors can cheer you up, while others can help you relax.

Knowing the effect of each essential oil can successfully solve a particular problem.

Usually, essential oils bear the names of the plants from which they are extracted, and the full power of this plant is embedded in them.

The following is a list of essential oils by names indicating the actions of the oils:

7.1. Sandal oil

It rejuvenates, revives, brightens, tones the skin, eliminates acne, skin itching, smoothes wrinkles and eliminates flabby skin. Effective for the care of dry, cracked, and defatted skin. It has an anti-cellulite effect. Helps to avoid impulsive actions and calms after stress. This is one of the flavors of meditation, eliminates tearfulness and insomnia. It has a favorable effect on health and general well-being. Stimulates the brain and helps focus. It is used in the treatment of angina and a runny nose.

7.2. Rose oil

Helps reduce anxiety. Its antioxidant properties can help treat acne and improve complexion to give an overall younger look. Moisturizes and strengthens the skin. When used in the composition of massage oil, it removes the feeling of fatigue and tension. It promotes smoothing of the skin, increases elasticity and eliminates inflammation, irritation, peeling, and scarring. It also helps smooth wrinkles, especially under the eyes. Excellent care for the any skin type, especially dry, withering and sensitive skin. It helps with acne and herpes.

7.3. Hyssop oil

This earthen, herbal, and fragrant essential oil can be used on the skin to minimize scarring, reduce inflammation, and act as a common healing agent.

7.4. Anise oil

It has a bactericidal, antiseptic, deodorizing effect. It reduces the number of microbes on the skin. It gives the skin elasticity and normalizes the water-fat balance of the epidermis. An excellent means for stimulating the body and increasing resistance to infections. Increases the elasticity of flabby skin. It helps with the struggles of depression and stress, eliminates and hyper excitability. Effective use in combination with lavender oils, patchouli, cloves, and citrus oils. It is combined with oils: fennel, cardamom, dill, cedar, cumin, coriander, rose tree, noble laurel, petitgrain and mandarin.

7.5. Orange Oil

It has antiseptic, antitoxic, deodorizing and antidepressant properties. It is soothing and refreshing. It regulates carbohydrate and fat metabolism, has a powerful anti-cellulite effect and stimulates the regeneration of skin cells. Rich in vitamins A, B and C. It has a lot of useful skincare properties when applied topically. This oil is contained in a variety of cosmetics, and it promises to make the skin brighter, smoother, and cleaner. It is most effective when used in combination with geranium oils, nutmeg sage, lavender, ylang-ylang, and citrus. The aroma of orange tones the nervous system improves performance, stabilizes the mood, fights with sadness and anxiety, helps to increase optimism and faith in one's own strength. It can also help with pain relief, is great for providing power and energy. Also, it tones the mind at the expense of its refreshing smell.

7.6. Jojoba oil

Jojoba oil is obtained from the seeds of wild jojoba shrubs, a small woody desert plant growing in Arizona, California, and Northwestern Mexico. Jojoba oil is very useful for the skin. Researchers found that jojoba oil accelerates wound healing at the cellular level. Historically, Native Americans have used jojoba oil to heal wounds. Jojoba oil contains unique fatty acids and esters of fatty alcohols. To improve skin appearance and reduce acne, include jojoba oil in your skincare procedure. Evidence indicates that clay masks with jojoba oil can be an effective remedy for mild acne.

7.7. Basil oil

 It has an antibacterial, softening and stimulating effect. It is recommended for the care of any type of skin. An excellent tonic and refreshing remedy. It has many useful properties from the skin to the internal application. It has been proven to have both antiviral and anti-inflammatory effects, so it can act as a remedy for colds and influenza, as well as for muscle relaxation. It has also been found to treat acne and even work as a way to reduce stress. It is recommended for use to combat anxiety, nervousness, and negligent fear. You can also add it to hair care treatments to give a glossy finish.

7.8. Jasmine oil

It has a stimulating effect. When applied topically, jasmine oil increases vigor, respiratory rate, and energy. These effects can contribute to improved mood and well-being.

7.9. Bergamot oil

It has a powerful soothing, antidepressant, antiseptic, tonic, and refreshing effect. It normalizes the secretion of sebaceous and sweat glands in fatty areas of the skin, brightens, and narrows the pores. Effective use in combination with lemon oils, lavender, juniper, geranium and citrus oils.

7.10. Clove oil

It has an antiseptic, anti-inflammatory and tonic effect. Baths with the addition of this oil help restore strength after nervous and physical overwork, benefit the skin by cleansing it. It is a traditional treatment for toothache. Boosts the immune system, improves the cardiovascular and respiratory systems, and improves digestion. It also stimulates mental activity. It is effective in combination with lavender oils, nutmeg sage, bergamot and ylang-ylang.

7.11. Grapefruit oil

It has cleaning, tonic, refreshing and antiseptic properties. It is effective against cellulite. Lightens and bleaches oily skin and narrows pores. Restores the natural secretion of sebaceous glands. Strengthens the nervous system and removes feelings of fear and irritation. It has a more bitter aroma, and it is a popular oil to use in a sprayer. It has antifungal properties that can help reduce harmful bacteria.

7.12. Ylang-ylang oil

 This flower oil emits a spicy but sweet aroma and has been proposed as a relaxation aid, self-assessment builder, and it can even act as a repellent in relation to certain insects. This is common in cosmetics and promises a list of cosmetic beneficial properties, including treating combination skin and stimulating hair growth. It relieves emotional tension, relieves anxiety and stimulates sexual desire. As well as strengthening hair and nails, it helps slow down the aging process of the skin, stimulates the growth of new cells and gives the skin elasticity, and tenderness. It is used to care for dry, coarse and peeling skin, it also cleans pores and removing toxic substances. Baths with the addition of ylang-ylang oil are recommended to stimulate the immune system. The most effective use is in combination with rosewood oils, bergamot.

7.13. Lavender oil

This incredibly popular oil has all kinds of useful properties. This delicate floral fragrance can help people relax and sleep. Moreover, inhaling it has been found to help manage headaches, while topical oil use can help reduce itching and swelling from insect bites.

It eliminates excitation, insomnia, depression and tearfulness. It has antiseptic, deodorizing, anti-burn and anti-inflammatory properties. Lavender oil is priceless for skincare, thanks to its rejuvenating power. It is used for the skin care of any type, especially for sensitive skin, the skin of the hips, buttocks and upper chest. It is also an oil that helps to communicate with people and correctly formulate and express their thoughts. It is effective in combination with cloves, geranium, patchouli, nutmeg sage, rosemary and citrus.

7.14. Juniper oil

Increases mental activity and has a calming effect. It has antiseptic, anti-inflammatory and tonic properties. It cleanses and refreshes acne prone and oily skin, promotes its regeneration, enhances blood circulation and prevents the emergence of vascular "stars." This oil increases skin elasticity, eliminates stretching, and cellulite. It is effective against itching and irritation from an insect bite.

7.15. Mint oil

Mint oil restores strength and has an antiseptic stimulating effect. It refreshes and awakens the skin and wipes traces of fatigue and lack of sleep from the skin. It also increases the protective functions of the epidermis, giving the skin elasticity, and tenderness. It has a cleansing effect on the skin. It is effective in the treatment of itchy skin, dermatitis, acne and the expansion of capillaries. Baths with the addition of mint oil eliminate nervousness. It is widely used for digestive disorders, as well as colds and viral diseases, and it also facilitates recovery from sunburn. It is effective for stress, depression and mental overstress. It helps to cope with nausea and dizziness and is also relaxing and soothing. It puts the heart in order and optimizes cerebral circulation. It is used in the treatment of skin and oral diseases. The use of essential mint oil is especially useful for oily skin. It is most effective in combination with lavender, bergamot, eucalyptus and citrus oils. It provides protection against unwanted insects and bite relief.

7.16. Neroli oil

It has a calming and antiseptic effect. It rejuvenates, revives weary, mature skin and smoothens wrinkles. It eliminates skin irritation and has a small vascular pattern. It promotes skin regeneration, strengthens hair and increases its elasticity.

7.17. Petitgrain oil

It has antiseptic, regenerating and soothing properties. It is recommended for dry, mature, and sensitive skin care. This oil smoothens wrinkles and contributes to increased elasticity of the skin.

7.18. Patchouli oil

It causes a surge of cheer and optimism, has an antidepressant effect and stimulates sexual desire. It has antiseptic, antitoxic, stimulating and deodorizing properties. It nourishes, smoothens, and renews dry, tired skin, promotes rapid regeneration and epithelization, eliminates a flabby bust, abdomen and hips. A bathtub with patchouli oil has a general strengthening effect and increases the body's resistance to infections. It is effective in combination with clove oils, bergamot and nutmeg sage.

7.19. Rosemary oil

Rosemary oil strengthens and activates the nervous system, relieving physical and mental fatigue, and apathy. It has deodorizing and tonic properties. Reduces sebum secretion, aligns the relief of the skin, restores the elasticity of the epidermis, prevents the emergence of vascular "sprockets." It is used for the care of oily and acne prone skin. It also stimulates the body's defenses. It is effective in combination with the oils of geranium, lavender, nutmeg and sage.

7.20. Tea tree oil

It is a powerful stimulator of mental activity. It helps to restore the body after stress, relieves excitement and promotes concentration. It has a powerful antiseptic and anti-inflammatory effect. It is used for purulent skin lesions, acne and for the relief of fatigue in the legs. It also has a regenerating and rehabilitating effect. It helps treat eczema, weaken reactions in people allergic to nickel, and even treats staphylococcal infections and insect bites. Bathing with the addition of tea tree oil helps restore strength after nervous and physical overwork, benefits the skin and cleanses it.

7.21. Nutmeg sage oil

It has an antiseptic, deodorizing and tonic effect. It is used for the skincare of any type of skin and is effective at returning life to withering skin. It is effective in combination with the oils of geranium, lavender and citrus.

7.22. Fir oil

Fir oil tones up, increases endurance and life activity, relieves stress, and chronic fatigue. It contains more than 35 biologically active substances and stimulates immunity. It has an antiseptic and anti-inflammatory effect. Bathing with the addition of fir oil help restore strength after nervous and physical overwork. It benefits the skin by tightening and cleansing it. It is an excellent flavoring agent that eliminates unpleasant smells. It is effective in combination with rosemary, lemon, nutmeg and sage oils.

7.23. Eucalyptus oil

Restores psych emotional balance. It has antiseptic, anti-burn, anti-herpetic, regenerating, and anti-inflammatory effects. It helps with colds and positively affects the respiratory system, cleaning blocked sinuses. In addition, it eliminates inflammation and oily skin. Bathing with the addition of eucalyptus oil contributes to the restoration of strength after nervous and physical overwork, and it benefits the skin by cleansing it.

7.24. Chamomile oil

With a combination of a light floral and herbal flavor, this oil has the potential of being a reliable source of stress relief that will help you relax when diffused and inhaled through steam. It is a strong analgesic and anti-allergic agent and is often used for colds. It also reduces an elevated body temperature as well as healing cuts and wounds. It has a bactericidal and anti-inflammatory effect. It bleaches, calms, and eliminates allergic manifestations. Although this oil is excellent for calming the mind, it is equally useful for the skin and has been recognized as a reliable source for treating conditions such as inflammation and eczema. It is suitable for dry and sensitive skin and stimulates hair growth by nourishing, and helps brighten hair. The smell of chamomile calmly acts on the nervous system, eliminates irritability and normalizes sleep.

7.25. Melissa oil

It promotes rapid acclimatization, helps with depression, melancholy, irritability, and insomnia. It is an antiherpetic agent.

7.26. Carrot seed oil

It improves the complexion, tones, rejuvenates the skin and makes it more elastic. It helps to get rid of age-related pigment spots and is suitable for dry and aging skin. It allows you to get rid of problems caused by vitiligo (lack of pigmentation), eczema and psoriasis. It has a general healing effect in inflamed wounds, dry and stiff skin, scarring, and calluses. It can be perfectly combined with almond oil. It protects the skin from frost and wind as well as increasing resistance to respiratory diseases. Clears the mind, reduces stress, and helps to combat the feeling of devastation.

Warning: It is better to refrain from using this oil during pregnancy.

7.27. Nutmeg butter

Improves blood circulation and is useful for skin as a rejuvenating agent. It helps fight fungal diseases and stimulates the digestive tract.

7.28. Lemon oil

Provides a tide of strength and positive emotions when struggling with depression and contributes to concentration. It has an antiseptic, antimicrobial and a deodorizing effect. It is an effective remedy against wrinkles and is perfect for oily facial skin and hair. It also has a whitening property, smoothens the skin, softens the cornea of the skin and brightens the nail plates. It is also recommended for hand care and skincare after epilation. This citrus oil contains antioxidants that can help reduce inflammation, combat the source of anaemia, increase energy levels, and reduce nausea. It is effective in combination with the oils of bergamot, lavender, geranium and orange.

7.29. Incense oil

The aroma can smell like a censer for you in the church and it has all kinds of astringent, digestive, antiseptic, and disinfectant properties. Incense can prevent oral problems such as bad breath, toothache, caries, and mouth ulcers Research even suggests it could help improve skin health and fight skin cancer. It also promotes normal cell growth.

7.30. Myrrh oil

It is believed that this aromatic essential oil treats skin problems that cause acne and cracked skin, and can even help in the treatment of the athlete's foot and skin cancer. In addition, it helps prevent sunburn.

7.31. Vetiver oil

Vetiver, this sweet aroma is often used in sedative aromatherapy to lift your overall mood and calm your nerves. As for its antioxidant properties, it has been recognized as contributing to skin health and scar healing. In addition, it perfectly moisturizes skin prone to aging by filling it with vitality.

7.32. Cedar oil

Earthen and naturally smelling cedar wood is used for a number of thematic cosmetic procedures. Studies have shown that these beneficial properties include controlling acne, treating eczema, and reducing dandruff. Cedar oil also helps reduce arthritis and relieve coughs.

7.33. Tui oil

This lesser-known oil emits a woody aroma and helps drive the beetles away and reduces stress. Its main attractiveness is the ability to maintain a healthy and shining complexion.

7.34. Immortelle oil

This oil, which smells like a mixture of honey and hay, has antioxidant, antibacterial, antifungal, and anti-inflammatory properties that can help strengthen internal and external health. In relation to skin, studies have shown that it can help athletes in the treatment of their feet, acne, and psoriasis.

7.35. Oregano oil

This essential spice oil has antibacterial, antiviral, and antifungal properties that can help treat athletes' legs, bacterial infections, psoriasis, and warts. In one study, oregano was found to have strong antioxidant properties and could also help treat fever, respiratory symptoms, and skin cancer. Its spicy aroma with shades of herbal tendencies can be used in aromatherapy or applied topically.

7.36. Cassia oil

Derived from the cassia plant (cinnamon family), this oil has a warm and spicy aroma similar to real cinnamon, although a little sweeter. Unlike the cooling effect of mint oils, cassia oil warms the body, which can make people feel calm.

7.37. Leuzea oil

This essential oil helps to combat asthenic and depressive conditions very well, it is used when there is a general decline in strength, stress, and overwork. Two drops on a pillow before bedtime - and in the morning you will feel well-rested and awake: leuzea oil improves the quality of sleep itself. Therapeutically, leuzea oil helps relieve cramps, relax muscles, eliminating painful sensations in them and it also helps with nausea.

7.38. Pine oil

 Pine oil has pronounced anti-inflammatory properties, it facilitates breathing, eliminates coughs, and helps in the removal of sputum. Inflammation of the respiratory system decreases and blood exchange in the lungs increases. A suffocating cough can be relieved by the active rubbing into the chest of a mixture of 30 ml of olive or coconut oil and 20 drops of pine oil, are very effective and inhalation will help in the treatment of bronchial asthma. Essential substances of pine oil help relax the body and restore the emotional state.

To relieve anxiety and irritation, you need to perform a very simple and effective exercise - apply several drops of pine oil to your palm, carefully rub and bring to your face vertically at a short distance. Take a deep breath, hold your breath for 10 seconds, and exhale slowly. Repeat several times within ten minutes. It is helpful to protect the internal forces of the body and relieve dizziness, migraine, and nausea, it is very good to use an aroma pendant with pine oil during the day.

7.39. Copaiba oil

Mined from the Amazonian plants of the genus Copaifera. Copaiba oil contains copalic acid, which stops the growth of common but harmful dental bacteria such as Streptococcus pyogenus, Streptococcus salivarius, and Streptococcus mutagens. Copaiba oil also has a strong anti-inflammatory effect. Copaiba oil also helps prevent or alleviate swelling in the body.

7.40. Valeriana oil

Helps with menopausal symptoms, especially sleep disorders. It sharpens the memory and increases the ability to solve emerging problems.

7.41. Pomegranate oil

 It is extremely rich in linolenic acid and essential fatty acids. Research suggests pomegranate oil may even delay the development of colon cancer and skin cancer. This oil also strengthens the immune system.

7.42. Sesame oil

 It has moisturizing properties, which makes it a favorite ingredient in skin and hair care products. However, its positive properties go beyond beauty. Sesame oil has a small sunscreen factor, contains fatty acids that reduce stress levels and blood pressure, and even slows down the growth of cancer in cells.

7.43. Geranium oil

Used in the fight against symptoms of premenstrual syndrome. Geranium oil is known for its astringent properties, which allows it to be used to freshen the skin, when reducing inflammation and stopping hemorrhages. It is used to treat acne, skin fat, accelerates circulation and reduces bloating. This oil can reduce scars and wrinkles and remove unpleasant body odors.

7.44. Black pepper oil

It may not smell as sweet as many oils, but black pepper oil still has a worthy place in the arsenal of natural medicine. Black pepper is widely used as a seasoning, and in particular because of its medicinal properties, including digestive care, treatment of seizures and convulsions, muscle warming, joint pain relief, arthritis, and treatment of bacterial infections.

We need to remember! No essential oil is ever used in

its pure form, and it is never to be mixed with water.

It is not recommended to use essential oils in an undiluted form, as pure concentrates can harm the body and human skin.

It is impossible to dilute essential oils with water since the structure of the oil molecules will not dissolve in water.

The very name "essential oil" speaks of its fat-like state and volatility. Fats as is widely known, do not dissolve in water. A thin film is created on the surface of the liquid. Fats in water can be emulsified by shaking in a closed container or by strong stirring, breaking the fat film into small drops. Without shaking and strong stirring, a finer-dispersed emulsion is made using auxiliary emulsifiers.

Pure essential oils are rather caustic substances that can cause chemical burns to the skin and mucous membranes. The essential oils are not diluted (soluble in alcohol), and only according to the formulation are added dropwise per dose of emulsifier, and then the oil-impregnated emulsifier is dissolved in water.

In medicine and cosmetology, there is a so-called base for oils. The base can be honey, milk, olive oil, wax, cream, masks, lotions, base oils, cream, bath salts, and so on.

The ether oils are added in a small amount to these bases.
It all depends on the method of use and the field of application.

For therapeutic purposes, essential oils can be used externally, by mixing drops with any ointment, like vaseline, and inwardly. For example, the essential oil of an orange lemon can be used with tea, before dropping 2-3 drops of oil into a teaspoon of sugar. An antiseptic working solution of essential oil can be prepared by using culinary salt as an emulsifier. For aromatic baths and aromatic lamps, the same emulsification principle is used.

Chapter 2: Use of essential oils

For thousands of years, people have been extracting essential oils from plants that are used in various elements of human life. Over time, the experience of obtaining and applying becomes more understandable, because each oil, in addition to an unsurpassed aroma, has its own unique effect on the human body. Essential oils are not just banal aromas, but real biologically active substances that can act on the human body in a wide range - from a useful effect on mental performance, psyche, mood, to a healing effect for a number of different diseases and pathologies.

Each oil has its own peculiarities. Some calm the nervous system, others excite. Certain species are used for inhalations for colds. Others serve as an excellent means of rejuvenation, they are actively added to cream and masks for skin and hair care.

Perhaps it is impossible to unequivocally answer the question of what odors essential oils contain. Their variety is great, but it is easy to find almost any pleasant

smell that exists in nature:
- sweet flavors
- acidic
- floral
- spicy
- calm;
- bright and varied.

When using vegetable essential oils, you need to study the precautions and basic rules. First of all, choose the right essential oil for yourself, the smell of which you really like.

The basic oils - coconut, jojoba, avocado, argan, and others - will help to provide comfortable application. Before use, several drops of essential oil can be added to the base oil, and only after mixing can it be applied to the skin or hair. Please note that it is not possible to apply internally without seeking permission from a physician.

Essential oils can be mixed and whole aroma compositions can be created.

The range of essential oils is quite wide. They also help in cosmetic purposes and treat diseases. Aromatherapy and bathing with essential oils can work wonders. Nature gives us the best and the properties of oils are unique. You can heal wounds and put your nerves in order. The main thing is to observe the dosage, test before applying to allergic reactions, and remember all the precautions. Then essential oils will bring only benefit and pleasure.

1. Aromatherapy

Aromatherapy (flavor treatment) is one of the simple and affordable methods in which essential oils reveal their therapeutic properties most favorably to the human body. This method allows you to improve, prevent, and treat various diseases. The introduction of the method into the human body can be carried out in various ways - through the airways, skin and mucous membranes.

Aromatherapy is the art of healing the body and the state of mind with essential oils. This is the most popular area of non-traditional medicine today. The conceptual basis of modern aromatherapy is the impact on the entire human body as a whole.

An unconventional medicine is based on the effects of external factors that positively affect the person.

There are special lamps, candles, stones, and other devices. This procedure requires careful oil selection and time. For example, if you pour tonic oil into a lamp overnight, then this can interfere with sleep and using a soothing oil in the morning can lead to feeling drowsy all day.

There are special bags with essential oils added to them. These bags are usually placed on a shelf with linen or on a bedside table so that the oil is healthy and strong.

Aromatherapy refers to one of the tools of non-standard treatment. Ether vapors enter the blood through the human airway, so they are absorbed by the body through a sense of smell. This is the essence of aromatherapy.

For the treatment procedure, a certain oil is selected. For the result to have a positive effect, you will need to know the types of essential oils. Each group is unique. One type works as an agent of activity and specifically activates the brain. Other treatments have a relaxing effect.

Some oil types are used for rejuvenating procedures and the manufacture of cosmetic creams. Others - for the treatment of infections, viruses and increased immunity.

An essential oil may have several characteristics. For example, using essential mint oil for aromatherapy, you can get a stimulating, refreshing, strengthening and tonic effect. For example, when making aromatic mixtures, it is necessary to take into account the effect of each component, to avoid using tonic and soothing oils in one composition.

Essential oils are useful only if all instructions for use and dosage are followed. Thanks to new technologies, it is possible to constantly explore and extract new oils. The range of their applications is constantly expanding.

1.1. Inhalations

Every year, with the advent of cool and rainy weather, the season of colds or acute respiratory diseases begins, affecting mainly the airways of the human body. Since essential oils have a safe and healing effect through the olfactory receptors of the nasal mucosa, it is possible to cope with colds using home aromatherapy.

Due to the bactericidal properties of most types of essential oils - unpleasant sensations that arise in the throat or in the form of nasal congestion can be eliminated. Essential oils of conifers have effective preventive properties, and essential oils of eucalyptus, lavender, rosemary, tea tree, niaouli , majorana, thyme, manuka and bergamot reveal themselves in treatment.

The first rule of home aromatherapy against a cold is the correct dosage of essential oils. To prevent the deterioration of general health and not get a burn, carefully study the instructions for the use of essential oils.

Inhalation with the addition of essential oils is a great way to get rid of cold, flu and bronchitis. It is often used for facial cleansing, strengthening immunity and simply for prevention.

Inhalations can be cold and hot. If the procedures are carried out regularly, it is better to purchase a special inhaler.

People with serious respiratory diseases should only inhale with the permission of doctor.

The following methods are quite simple in their execution, but at the same time they will effectively help to get rid of the cold:

✓ Hot inhalations: In order to carry out this method, it is not necessary to purchase a special inhaler device. Boil the kettle and pour about 1 liter of boiling water into the prepared bowl. Then add up to 4 drops of aromatic essential oil are added to the water, for example, fir or mixtures of several species - fir, mint and rosemary. Anis, thyme, citrus fruits are also recommended for colds. With a large towel, create a protective dome above your head and breathe in the fragrant steam for 7 minutes. When the solution is inhaled, the airways are cleaned, immunity is strengthened and skin is cleaned. Such inhalations must be performed two to three times a day, one of which must be performed before bedtime.

✓ Cold inhalations. A simple method that requires a handkerchief or napkin or a piece of fabric and essential oils. Only 2-3 drops of essential oil are applied on the handkerchief, after which its aromatic pairs are inhaled several times a day. Inhale the smell for 5-10 minutes. Try to breathe smoothly, slowly and deeply.

1.2. Aroma lamp

The simplest and most popular aromatherapeutic method in the treatment of colds. An aroma lamp is located in the room in which the patient is constantly located. To carry out this process, hot water is added to the glass container followed by 5 drops of essential oil such as eucalyptus or mint. The course of therapeutic procedures should be carried out daily for half an hour until full recovery.

Alternatively, an ultrasonic diffuser can be purchased in which essential oils can be added and a similar effect of the procedure can be obtained.

1.3. Aroma lamp with candle

When using an aroma lamp, you must first pour hot water into it, light a special candle and only then add oil. Depending on the type of ether, the number of drops varies from 1 to 3.

Aromatization of the room is carried out by pre-closing all windows and doors. Aroma lamps should not be lit for more than 20 minutes.

1.4. Compresses

They are used for joint, muscle pain, as well as back pain. Compressed oil is selected based on the desired result. It can be used to relieve inflammation, pain relief, or cramping. Compresses, like inhalations, consist of two types - cold and hot. Cold ones are used for bruises, sprains, tumors and warm compresses are recommended to remove inflammation, to treat chronic diseases such as rheumatism, radiculitis and osteochondrosis. For example, dermatitis, neurodermatitis, tissue microcirculation disorders, burning, and swelling after insect bites - can be relieved with the help of a compress made with leuzea oil. It is necessary to apply compresses to affected areas of the skin (any neutral oil base plus 6-7 drops of Leuzea oil) or even make wet wraps using a sheet: take 10-12 drops of Leuzea oil for 500 ml of warm water and shake thoroughly.

The most useful feature of aromatherapy is the ability to use it independently at home. This method cannot completely replace classical medicine for serious diseases and disorders of the body. Methods of home aromatherapy are closely related to methods for treating colds. Only the choice of essential oil is different, the properties of which will help create the atmosphere you need. For example, a relaxing environment can be created with chamomile or lavender oil. If you want to create a more cozy and warming environment then use orange or cardamom oil. Rose or sandal oil is best to create a romantic atmosphere and for mental balance and harmony melissa and neroli oils are best.

Problems or trouble at work? Drip a few drops of essential oil into the aroma lamp. Essential oils can return a good disposition of the spirit and rid you of bad thoughts, for example:

- Irritation and nervousness: lavender, geranium, melissa and neroli.
- Depression and grim thoughts: bergamot and grapefruit.
- Fear: rose, orange and jasmine.

Aromatherapy has a direction of a healing effect on the human body. The constituent components of oils have high bioactivity, so they are useful only when used correctly. A certain process fits a particular oil, therefore it is necessary to select responsibly. Use without excess, strictly follow the prescribed dosage.

By competently using essential oils, it is possible to

eliminate negative factors affecting the body (physical, psychological). Benefits will include an increased mood and activity, as well as strengthened immunity. As a result there will be a general harmonious state and excellent well-being.

2. Aromatic bath, sauna, massage

2.1. Bath

Taking a bath with an incredible aroma after a long day at work is a great way to relax, relieve tension, fatigue and stress. Bathing also relieves muscle tensions, after training.

During the winter and cold months, lemon or pine aroma is used. To relieve stress or psychological stress, rose oil, geranium and lavender is recommended. Juniper oil will help relieve muscle tension.

It is possible to follow the recommendations for each type of skin. It is better to select the appropriate essential oil, for example:

- Dry skin - neroli or geranium;
- Oily skin - citrus fruits;
- Problem skin - tea tree, lavender and lemon.

Before adding essential oils to the filled bath, it is necessary to mix them with any base oil, milk, or sea salt. In this way, you will avoid skin irritation and allergic reaction. The following proportions are suitable: for 1 teaspoon of base oil, add no more than 4 drops of essential oil, for example, tea tree. Or per 100 gr of sea salt (milk) - up to 15 drops of a mixture of lavender and mayorana. The maximum time for the bath should be 15 minutes.

Bath Rules:
- Take a shower before taking a bath;
- The water temperature should be between 36-39 degrees;
- Do not use additional products; such as gel, shampoo or foam;
- The base for the oil is often milk, honey, salt and kefir;
- The bath duration should be between 5-20 minutes, not more than three times a week;
- After bathing, do not rinse and wipe dry.

The bath water should not be burning hot, otherwise, the ethers will quickly fly away, and you will not receive the benefit of the procedure.

An example of a soothing bath: for the best effect, take three drops of Leuzea oil and mix with an emulsifier such as milk, cream, or honey, carefully spread in warm water. After 20 minutes in such a bath, you will feel much better, and your nerves will be much calmer.

2.2. Sauna

Oils in the sauna are used to improve breathing and to prevent diseases of the respiratory tract. The most popular oils are eucalyptus, spruce and cedar oil. They are added to a ladle of water, the resulting solution is poured onto hot stones (if these stones are available and it is not forbidden to water them).

2.3. Massage

Essential oils are also used in therapeutic massage, but, as in other procedures, they are only pre-mixed with other oils when applied to the skin. To do this, you will need 25 ml of any base oil, for example, olive, 9-10 drops of rosemary essential oil or a mixture of several essential oils - rosemary, fir and mint. Apply a mixture of oils to the skin of the back, chest and legs with long, pulling movements and while deeply inhaling fragrant fumes. The procedure can be performed in a day.

A properly made massage itself has healing properties, and using essential oils has an amazing effect. The massage oil is selected based on the desired result:

- ✓ to relieve joint pains- the aroma of nutmeg;
- ✓ to break down adipose tissues - citrus;
- ✓ cloves are good for warming up and improving blood circulation;
- ✓ the lifting effect is achieved with rose oil or jasmine;
- ✓ the base is most often body or face oils.

An example of an anti-stress massage: you need to prepare a mixture of three drops of Leuzea oil, two drops of lavender dissolved in sesame oil, olive or coconut oil - take about a tablespoon. This mixture must be rubbed into the area of the crown, the back of the head and temples.

When choosing essential oil you need to focus not only on its properties, but also on the smell as it must be pleasant to the person to whom the massage is done. After the procedure, you should not go outside for about an hour.

The combination of massage and aromatherapy has a beneficial effect on the respiratory organs and skin. During aromatic massage, blood circulation improves, lymph stalls accelerate, and the work of all organs improves.

3. Essential oils in cosmetology

The properties of essential oils allow them to be successfully used in cosmetology. Properly selected esters, taking into account a particular type of skin and therefore benefit its condition. Essential oils increase the life potential and energy of skin cells, which helps counter negative environmental factors and aging.

Some essential oils fight free radicals and interfere with the aging process throughout the body.

The properties of essential oils in cosmetology are manifested in improving the condition of the skin and hair. Assets are used in professional and home cosmetology by enriching cosmetics with them. They are added to finished cosmetic products or self-prepared masks immediately before use.

If you add several drops of essential oil to a prepared bath or mask, the benefit will only increase. At the same time, you need to be careful and be able to navigate among the entire variety of plant essential oils, as if they are misapplied, they can be harmful to the body.

Oils are recommended to be added to the cosmetic product just before application to the skin.

Essential oils may be added to the care routine by adding several drops to the substrate, such as a facial cream or base oil. When applying the obtained essence to the skin, the oils penetrate much deeper into the layers of the skin. Ethers will help to transport useful substances to skin cells faster and strengthen the cosmetic product several times. The exception is tea tree oil, experts recommend using it in its pure form and locally.

The following essential oils are isolated:

- Essential oils of rose, chamomile, neroli, geranium, lavender, jasmine, lemon combined with base oils are suitable for normal skin. Basic oils can be jojoba, almond, macadamia, apricot, or grape bone oil.

- Essential oils of lavender, geranium, orange, incense, jasmine, sandal, blue tansy, majorana, rosewood combined with base oils are used for dry skin. Base oils for dry skin: macadamia, almond, jojoba, apricot bones and rosehip.

- Essential oils of bergamot, lemon, grapefruit, ylang-ylang, ginger, patchouli, cypress, cedar, juniper, melissa, rosemary, tea tree are used for oily skin. Base oils for oily skin: apricot or grape bones - in combination with the above essential oils normalize sebaceous glands.

- For problematic skin, the essential oils of jasmine, lavender, juniper, bergamot, tea tree, ylang-ylang, lemon, geranium, lemongrass, cloves, orange, chamomile are used. Base oils for problematic skin: jojoba, wheat embryos, sweet almonds. Verbena, cypress, lemon, myrtle, mint, neroli, roses will help to get rid of couperose.

- The essential oils of chamomile, tea tree, mandarin, neroli, blue tansy, ylang-ylang, patchouli are suitable for sensitive skin. Base oils for sensitive skin include: apricot bones, calendula, rice bran and babassu.

- For mature skin, essential oils of lavender, immortal, rosemary, lemon, patchouli, oregano, roses, sage, carrots are used. Base oils for mature skin include: argans, jojoba, evening primrose, cocoa and grant seeds.

- Essential oils of grapefruit, ylang-ylang, lemon, majorana, myrtle, melissa, rosemary will help to clean and narrow the pores.
- To return a beautiful complexion and saturate the skin with vitamins; the essential oils of verbena, limette, rose, mint, neroli, rose tree, orange, bigardia, verbena and spruce will help.

The main rule is to select an ether taking into account the type of skin and not exceed the dosage.

Depending on the type of skin, you can use different recipes for cosmetics.

3.1. Oily Skin Care

Add 3 drops of sandal essential oil, 2 drops of grapefruit and 1 drop of melissa to 10 ml of finished cream.

For oily skin with wide pores: add 2 drops of lemon oil and 1 drop of mint, neroli and eucalyptus to the finished cream.

Masks for oily skin:
1. Mix a tablespoon of ground oat flakes with two spoons of nettle decoction, add 4 drops of bergamot and 3 drops of grapefruit.
2. 2 tablespoons of white clay are mixed with warm water to sour cream consistency. Add 1 teaspoon of honey. A 1 drop of essential oils of juniper and lemon is added to the obtained mixture of clay and honey. It is distributed on the face, left until dry and washed with warm water.

Tonic for oily skin: add 3 drops of chamomile oil, geranium and orange to 10 ml of alcohol. Add 90 ml of pure water or grass decoction. Wipe the skin of each wash with the resulting composition.

3.2. Dry Skin Care

Add 4 drops of rose oil and 3 drops of chamomile to 10 ml of base oil, for example, peach or wheat germs. Apply this mixture to your face in the morning and evening instead of cream.

Dry skin mask:
1. Mix 15 grams of white clay with chamomile decoction. Add 5 ml of rosehips oil, 3 drops of rose oil and 1 drop of orange.
2. To warm base oil in the amount of 1 teaspoon (rice bran, almond, jojoba) 2 drops of sandal and rosewood and 1 drop of jasmine are added. The composition is applied to the face for 30 minutes. The remains are removed with a wet napkin.

Mask for peeling skin: mix 5 ml of liquid honey, a tablespoon of sour cream, 6 drops of cardamom oil.

Oil mixtures for caring for tender skin around the eyes: add 1 drop of essential sandal oil, roses and lavender to 10 ml of macadamia oil; add 1 drop of neroli oil and 2 drops of sandal to 10 ml of sweet almond oil; add 1 drop of vitamin A, E, essential oils of jasmine and rose to 10 ml of apricot bone oil.

3.3. Mask for normal skin type care

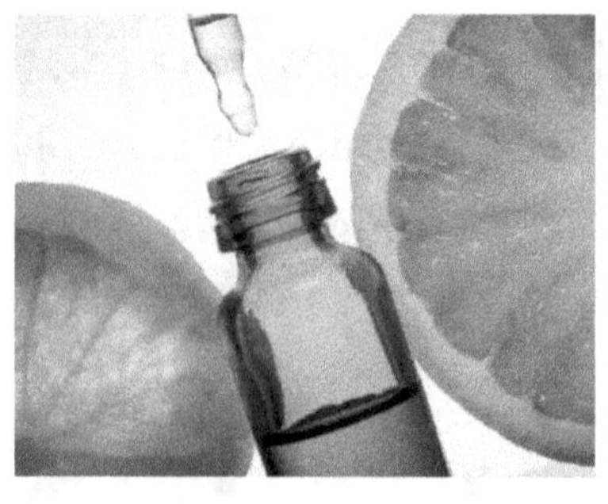 1 teaspoon of base oil of apricot, peach or grape bones is enriched with grapefruit and mint esters of 1 drop.
An alternative can be rose or lavender.

It is applied for 20 - 30 minutes, the residues are removed with a wet napkin.

3.4. Care for problematic skin prone to rashes

Mix 10 ml of finished cream with 2 drops of juniper oil, 1 drop of pine oil and 2 drops of lavender oil.

Instead of the finished cream, you can use light oil that does not clog pores, for example, grape bone oil.

Mix 10 ml of cream or grape oil with 2 drops of eucalyptus oil, 2 drops of lemon oil and 1 drop of incense.

Mask for problematic skin: mix a teaspoon of honey, half a teaspoon of alcohol, half a teaspoon of water, add 2 drops of essential grapefruit oil and tea tree.

3.5. Withering Skin Care

Add 1 drop of essential oil of fennel, mint, nutmeg to 10 ml of base oil or finished cream.

Add 1 drop of essential oils of myrrh, incense, nutmeg and neroli to 10 ml of walnut oil.

Wrinkle smoothing mask: Mix a tablespoon of pea flour, a teaspoon of sour cream and add 1 drop of essential fennel oils and mint.

Mask against wrinkles: mix a tablespoon of jojoba oil, 4 drops of incense oil, 2 drops of vetiver and 1 drop of sandal.

You can always prepare an essence according to the type of your skin in advance. In accordance with the necessary proportions and instructions of the manufacturer, it is necessary to mix the oils. Then place the resulting contents in a glass vessel and store in a dark place. Thus, you can use the oil essence immediately without preparation. An alternative will be ready-made cosmetics, which in their composition contain a concentration of essential oils.

Very often essential oils are added to professional

cosmetics. Based on the oil property, cosmetics have different indications for use. During the selection of the extract, it is necessary to consult with a beautician.

3.6. List of essential oils to solve various skin problems

- Orange - eliminates greasy gloss.
- Bergamot - narrows pores, tones, brightens skin.
- Geranium - tones.
- Cloves - restores the structure of young skin, anti-inflammatory.
- Grapefruit - normalizes the functioning of sebaceous glands, narrows and bleaches the pores of the skin.
- Ilang-ilang - reassuring.
- Ginger - tones.
- Cypress - eliminates greasy gloss.
- Lavender - calming, from wrinkles.
- Lemon - tones, from wrinkles.
- Chinese lemon - narrows and brightens the pores of the skin.
- Limette - eliminates greasy gloss.
- Melissa - tones, calms, has an anti-inflammatory property.
- Myrrh - eliminates fat gloss.
- Juniper - tones, has a disinfectant property.
- Mint tones, eliminates greasy gloss.
- Neroli - eliminates greasy gloss.
- Patchuli is reassuring.
- Petitgrain - has an antioxidant and regenerative effect.
- Rose tree - eliminates greasy gloss.
- Rosemary - tones.
- Chamomile - calming.
- Chabretz - tones.

- Tea tree - soothing.

Rosemary, thyme, sage, lavender are useful for healing wounds.

3.7. Hair care

There are many recipes that are prepared independently with the addition of essential oils. These may be face or hair masks and body lotions. Hair masks are particularly popular.

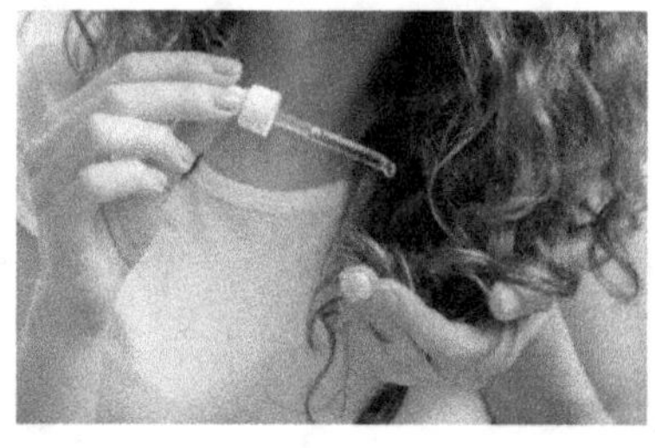

Oil nourishes hair, removes dryness, brittleness, restores color. When preparing yourself, you need to follow all the instructions very clearly so as not to harm your body.

The benefits and harms of essential hair oils are manifested, depending on the literacy of their use, in improving, accelerating growth, getting rid of dandruff and giving brilliance.

Essential oils are used in masks, added to shampoos and rinses, the dosage is not more than1 drop.

For masks, base oils are the basis, the benefits of which are different, depending on the properties of each of them.

For hair care, choose essential oils according to the type

of hair and the problem you intend to solve.

- ✓ For daily hair care, essential oils of rose, rosemary, grapefruit, lavender, sage, juniper, air, bergamot, lemon are suitable.

- ✓ For dry hair, the essential oils of lavender, sandal, orange, mandarin, chamomile, ylang-ylang, roses, myrrh, incense are suitable.

- ✓ For oily hair, choose essential oils of lemon, tea tree, mint, cedar, eucalyptus, verbena, ginger, rosemary, bergamot, sage.
  Manifestations of fatty seborrhea sesame, calendula and avocado are reduced.

- ✓ Essential oils are useful for reducing hair loss, which will not only suspend the process of hair loss, but also stimulate the growth of new hair. These include oils of rosemary, aira, ylang-ylang, tea tree, rose tree, mint, coriander, verbena, cedar and pine.
  Precipitation is reduced and argan and turnip are smoothed. Pine and forest nut oils have the same property.

- ✓ Pumpkin, castor, mustard oil is stimulated for hair growth.

✓ Essential oils of geranium, tea tree, rosemary, lavender, grapefruit, basil, cedar, poppy, peach, mustard, eucalyptus are suitable for dandruff control.

✓ Reduce the fragility of macadamia, avocado and hemp.

✓ Versatile oils that improve the condition in general are castor, linen, olive, jojoba.

Masks based on essential oils

- Normal hair masks:
1. Mix 15 ml of sea buckthorn oil with 7 drops of chamomile essential oil. Apply the oil mixture to the skin and hair before washing for 30 minutes, then rinse with shampoo.
2. Add a drop of essential oils of sage, rosemary, chamomile, and cedar to 15 ml of almond oil. Wipe the oils into the scalp with your fingertips, put on a polyethylene hat, and hold the mask for at least an hour.

- Oily hair masks:
1. Add 2 drops of essential oils of cedar, cypress, juniper, and lavender to one and a half tablespoons of jojoba oil. After 30 minutes, wash your head with shampoo and rinse with water acidified with lemon juice.

2. Mix together a tablespoon of honey, kefir, and bulb oil. Add two drops of essential oils of thyme, bergamot, rosemary, and lavender. This mask can be left on your hair from 30 minutes to two hours, the longer, the better.

- Dry hair masks:
1. Mix along a tablespoon of sesame oil, wheat germ oil, and avocado oil. Add one drop of essential oils of sage, nutmeg, ylang-ylang, carrot seeds, and chamomile. Oil wrapping can be done in the evening and left on the hair until morning.
2. Mix one egg, a tablespoon of natural vinegar, 2 tablespoons of macadamia oil, add 2 drops of any essential citrus oils.

The properties of essential hair oils are disclosed with regular use of useful components, at least 1 time a week.

3.8. A Brief Guide to Essential Oils

The use of essential oils depends on the presence of a problem:

With a heterogeneous skin color, the presence of freckles, pigment spots, lemon and grapefruit oils are used.

With "goose legs" around the eyes the essential oils sandal, limette, roses and neroli are known to help.

Essential oils of rose wood, ylang-ylang, orange will make the skin smooth, velvety, remove excessive gloss.

Cypress essential oil helps eliminate oily skin gloss.

If the vascular pattern is too visible on the skin of the face, the essential oils of cypress, lemon, lavender, mint, sage will help.

If the skin has been adversely affected and stressed, use the essential oils of rosewood, chamomile, rose, neroli and ylang-ylang.

If there are many pimples on the skin, comedones, pores are blocked, the essential oils of lemon, juniper, bergamot, chamomile will help.

Recommended doses of essential oils:

- To add 2-4 drops of essential oils to the base oils for facial care: 1 tablespoon of oil.
- To enhance the effectiveness of creams and lotions: up to 5 drops of essential oil per 10-15 ml of cream.
- For hair care: we take 4-6 drops of essential oils per 1 tablespoon of base (mask or oil).
- When taking care of the body: add 6-10 drops of essential oils to 1 tablespoon of base oil.
- For rinses: 2-3 drops of oil per cup of warm boiled water.
- To aromatize the house with aroma lamps: 3-4 drops of essential oil (added to water poured into the lamp cup) on 15 m2 of area.
- For baths: 4-7 drops of essential oils per bath, pre-dissolve in the base (milk, base oil, honey, cream, salt for baths).
- For massage: 3-6 drops of essential oil per 1 tablespoon (15 ml) of base oil.
- For sauna and baths: 2-4 drops of essential oil per 15 m2.

3.9. Essential oils for weight loss

Essential oils can be used to reduce weight, improve metabolism and reduce appetite. For this purpose aromatic compositions are used during a bath, a massage or wrapping. Oils can also be ingested or used in aroma lamp.

- To normalize metabolic processes and remove toxins from the body, use essential oils of grapefruit, lemon, ginger, rosemary, cypress, dill, geranium, juniper and cardamom.

- Essential oils of rosemary, eucalyptus, cypress, geranium, grapefruit, juniper, lemon, sweet dill, cardamom, ginger, laurel and tui will help to remove excess liquid from the body and enhance lymphocyte.

- To reduce appetite, inhale essential oils of mint, vanilla, cinnamon, cypress, lemon, orange and dill.

- Essential oils of cypress, anise, grapefruit, ylang-ylang, orange, lemon, jasmine, patchouli and mandarin will help tone down and tighten the skin. These same oils contribute to the rapid burning of fat if used during wrapping or massage.

- If you are on a diet and deny yourself harmful, but such delicious foods, then it is possible that you will encounter a phenomenon such as irritability. The essential oils of lavender, vanilla, calendula, cypress will help to calm nerves, relieve tension, and bring all their feelings to a state of rest and pacification.

Aromatic composition for weight loss:

Mix 10 drops of cypress essential oil and 9 drops of juniper with 5 tablespoons of jojoba oil. Rub this mixture into the skin with massaging movements, paying special attention to the hips and abdomen. The same composition may be added to a bath filled with warm water. For one procedure, it is enough to take 1 tablespoon of the mixture. If you want to not only tighten but smooth and exfoliate the skin, then add this composition to a handful of fine sea salt. Gently massage problem areas with this natural scrub. Sea salt will perfectly remove toxins and excess liquid from skin cells, jojoba oil will smooth the skin, and esters will give tone.

Clay wrapping for weight loss:

Dilute 3 tablespoons of black clay with warm water, add 10 ml of grape bone oil or almonds, and 8-10 drops of grapefruit essential oil. Apply a mask to the thighs, buttocks, and abdomen, wrap the treated areas with a film. You can wear warm hammocks or trousers to strengthen the action of the mask. After 1.5-2 hours, rinse with cool water and apply any cream with a tightening effect on the skin.

Ingestion of essential oils:

Mix 1 drop of essential juniper oil with a teaspoon of honey. Take this mixture every morning before eating, be sure to drink a lot of liquid. Juniper oil normalizes metabolism, removes excess liquid and has a diuretic effect.

3.10. Essential oils for cellulite

The most effective oils that help quickly solve the problem of cellulite are essential oils of orange, grapefruit, bergamot, lemon, mandarin, juniper, rosemary, geranium, cypress, vetiver and vanilla.

Mixtures of the above oils can be used for anti-cellulite massage, added to bathing water or mixed with already prepared industrial means, thereby enhancing their effect.

Anti-cellulite cream:
> Mix 1 tablespoon of sweet almond oil, 10 drops of essential grapefruit and bergamot oils, 8 drops of geranium oil, 6 drops of nutmeg oil, 3 drops of cinnamon oil. Apply oil cream to the thighs, buttocks, abdomen with strong rubbing movements. Massage can be carried out not only with your hands, but also with a special vacuum can, which can be bought at the pharmacy.

Anti-cellulite wrapping:
> Mix 50 ml of apple vinegar in half with water, add 3 drops of essential oils of mint, lemon and rosemary. Apply this solution to the problem areas, wrap them with film and wrap with a blanket. The duration of the procedure is 1 hour, after which you need to rush under a cool shower and apply any moisturizing cream and a drop of cinnamon essential oil to the skin.

Anti-cellulite bath:

Mix a glass of milk, 5 drops of essential oils of lemon and orange and a handful of sea salt. Dissolve this mixture in water and take a bath for 20-25 minutes.

Anti-cellulite massage:

Lubricate the skin with any base oil, then take a brush with hard bristles, drop of cinnamon or citrus oil. With circular movements, carefully study the whole body, from the feet to the neck. Massage must be done with effort so that the skin turns red and begins to heat up intensely.

3.11. Essential aphrodisiac oils

Essential oils have a positive effect on our emotional state. They can both relax a person and excite them. Essential aphrodisiac oils improve blood circulation in the pelvic organs, eliminate stagnation and bring muscles into tone. Skillfully selected essential oils or a mixture of essential oil can betray great confidence to a restrained man and a shy girl.

The most famous aphrodisiac oils are: bergamot, cloves, vetiver, jasmine, ylang-ylang, green coffee, cedar, cypress, cassia, cinnamon, muscat, sandal, myrrh, thyme, bigardia, rose, rosemary, patchouli, coriander, basil, velvets, violet, vanilla, cloves, coriander, limette, nutmeg, ginger, palmarose, tuberose, sage, fennel, verbena, grapefruit, rose tree, neroli, majorana, juniper, myrtle, citronella, cardamom, pine and geranium.

Aphrodisiac oils are divided into three groups:

- Soothing. Help relieve tension and relax: rose, ylang-ylang, sage, lavender, neroli.
- Stimulants. It's cinnamon, black pepper, cardamom, cedar. With these oils you need to be

careful and try not to overpower, since the effect may be the opposite of what you expect.
- Hormonal. These oils that affect hormone production include jasmine and sandalwood.

Among aphrodisiac oils, there is no clear gradation for male and female, you need to focus on whether you enjoy the aroma and what emotions it causes you.

To create an intimate mood, you can pre-aromatize the room with essential oils.

Light the aroma lamp or drop a drop of oil onto the candle, trying not to hit the wick. It is possible to aromatize the room using a pulverizer and a mixture of water, alcohol and 3-5 drops of any essential oil. To aromatize the room before love games, essential oils of patchouli, ylang-ylang, muscat, ginger or lemon are well suited. With the same oils, you can add to bedding by using several drops of sensual ethers to the water for the last rinse when washing the laundry.

Before a romantic date, take a bath of essential oils. The skin will acquire a light sensual aroma that your loved one will smell only by getting close to you. The thinner and more unobtrusive the aroma, the more exciting the effect on a partner it has. Baths with the essential oils of patchuli, neroli or ylang-ylang will help to wake up sensuality. These oils are considered the most powerful aphrodisiacs, equally strongly affecting both women and men. Essential oils can be added to the bath, either separately or by mixing several types. Add sandal, rose, bergamot or sage to the emulsifier by drop of essential oils. Focus on your own feelings about the mixture, it should cause pleasant associations.

Aphrodisiac oils can be used instead of perfumes.

 For the woman to feel like a sorceress; collect in one bottle 10 ml of base oil with 2 drops of jasmine, 2 drops of rose, 1 drop of sandal and 1 drop of bergamot. This magical mixture will not leave a single man indifferent.

But a man can make up a similar love perfume: mix 10 ml of almond oil, 3 drops of sandal, 2 drops of cedar and 1 drop of ylang-ylang and patchouli. Store these mixtures in a bottle of dark glass and apply to energy points before a romantic date.

Sensual mixture for erotic massage: mix 20 ml of almond or nut oil, 4 drops of rose oil, 2 drops of geranium oil and cinnamon. Apply this mixture to the whole body of your partner with gentle stroking movements, starting from the feet and gradually moving up. Make sure that the movements are smooth, and in especially sensitive places they are almost elusive.

4. Treatment with essential oils. Folk recipes

Everyone knows that essential oils are very useful. They are used not only for cosmetic purposes, but also for health purposes:

- **For bruises:** Apply to the bruise area with a mixture of oils: chamomile 2 drops, geranium 2 drops, lavender 1 drop. Dissolve in one teaspoon of vegetable oil.

- **In case of burns:** Treat the burn area with 1-5 drops of lavender oil and apply a sterile bandage.

- **For chills and heat:** Dissolve in 600 ml of cold water: eucalyptus 3 drops, peppermint 2 drops, lavender 2 drops, geranium 1 drop. Wet the napkin with a solution and put for 10 - 15 minutes on the forehead, elbow bends, inguinal and popliteal areas. Repeat the procedure for an hour 4 times, until the heat reduces.

- **For a cold:** Rinse the neck, back and chest with an oil solution of aromatic oils once a day: eucalyptus

5 drops, thyme 3 drops, tea tree 2 drops. One dessert spoon of vegetable oil.

- **For fractures:** After applying the immobilizing bandage, wet the bandage over the fracture site with a solution of oils: geranium 5 drops, tibia 3 drops, lavender 2 drops. Dissolve in one dessert spoon of vegetable oil.

- **For a headache:** Rub a solution of essential oils into the temporal regions: peppermint 3 drops, lavender 2 drops. Dissolve in one teaspoon of vegetable oil.

- **For insomnia:** Mixtures of essential oils for an aroma lamp and massage mixtures for active points (per 5 ml base oil). Mixtures: 4 drops of chamomile + 4 drops of lavender; 4 drops of nerol + 2 drops of geranium; 6 drops of majorana and add 2 drops of rosewood.

- **For operability:** Mixtures: 2 drops of basil + 1 drop of cypress + 2 drops of grapefruit; 3 drops of grapefruit + 2 drops of ginger; 2 drops of rosemary + 3 drops of bergamot; 2 drops of mint + 1 drop of incense + 2 drops of lemon.

- **For a cough.** Mixtures of essential oils for an aroma lamp and massage mixtures for rubbing

(15-20 ml base oil) 4 drops of mint; 3 drops of hyssop; 2 drops of eucalyptus; 2 drops of benzoin; 2 drops of thyme.

- **Essential oils for dry coughing.** For 15 ml of base oil (for massage of the back and chest): 2 drops of tea tree, 2 drops of incense, 4 drops of orange; 4 drops of eucalyptus, 2 drops of lavender, 1 drop of pine; 4 drops of sandal, 3 drops of lavender and 3 drops of cajuput.

- **Essential oils in wet coughing.** For 15 ml of base oil (for massage of the back and chest) 2 drops of pine needles, 2 drops of sandal, 2 drops of rosemary; 2 drops of tea tree, 3 drops of eucalyptus, 2 drops of fir; 2 drops of lavender, 3 drops of cloves, 3 drops of lemon and 2 drops of incense.

5. Accessories for essential oils

After you have found the right essential oils for yourself, why not buy some accessories? From bottle storage boxes and diffusers to items that will help you enjoy essential oils on the go, for example:

✓ A crate for your oils - if you find that your bottles of essential oil are starting to take up too much space, then you definitely need an organizer. The storage box can serve as a great way to track all your bottles, while being a beautiful addition to the decor of your home.

✓ Case - whether you only have a few oils you use daily, or travel with some of them you really like, a small bag will help keep up to 10 of them in place.

✓ Mini diffuser - always need a little aromatherapy on the go? The oil diffuser connects to your machine so that you can calm down on the way to a big meeting or increase the energy level on the way to lunch.

✓ Ultrasonic diffuser - for those who do not want a large, bulky diffuser, there are compact models of ultrasonic diffusers. Such a diffuser is pleasant both aesthetically and therapeutically. Just plug it in, and the steam will begin to emit beautiful light fog for everyone.

✓ An aromatic necklace- if you like to take aromatherapy wherever you go, a fashionable medallion is exactly what you need.

✓ Auxiliary bottles - glass bottles are a great way to store essential oils that you like to use in your favorite recipes. Pipettes facilitate measurement, and dark glass helps oils maintain their effectiveness.

6. Precautionary measures

Before using essential oils, it is necessary to study the rules and contraindications:

1. Essential oils are concentrates and require careful use, so they are diluted with base vegetable oils when applied to the skin. In pure form, only essential lavender oil and tea tree can be applied to the skin. All others can provoke a burn of the skin and mucosa.
2. Check in advance if you have an allergy to essential oil, for this you need to dilute a drop of essential oil with the base and apply it to the inside of the elbow if the skin remains clear for 24 hours, then it is is fine to use.
3. Begin using essential oils with minimal dosages, if you use an aroma lamp, then the duration of the first sessions is no more than 10 minutes. Do not exceed the dosage. If the instruction says that cinnamon essential oil needs to be taken 1-2 drops per 10 ml of base oil, then use that much. Exceeding the dosage is fraught with allergies or burns. If you are just starting to master aromatherapy, then reduce the recommended dose of essential oils by half. If after several

applications of negative reactions, allergies, unpleasant sensations do not occur, then you can safely use the full dose.

4. Some essential oils are toxic and cannot be ingested.
5. Some essential oils of citrus are phototoxic, so pigmentation may appear under the influence of the sun;
6. Buy "clean" essential oils. Among essential oils, there are all kinds of diluted versions and perfumes that do not have the properties of the pure essences.
7. After 21 days of oil use, take a break (1-2 weeks).
8. Focus on your own feelings. No matter how useful and miraculous the oil would be, but if you do not like its aroma, then it is very likely that you will not receive the benefit of aromatherapy.

7. Cooking and Beverage Preparation

There is no separate category of essential oils for addition to food. However, the manufacturer, as a rule, indicates on the packaging of the oil whether it can be ingested. It is worth noting that if you want to drink oil, then it should be of the highest quality, namely 100% pure, natural and whole. Due to the high concentration of essential oils, they can only be used as a food additive for a more effective impact on human health.

When entering the body, essential oils enter the bloodstream through the gastrointestinal tract, and then are transported throughout the rest of the body. Therefore, you should approach the selection and dosage of essential oil wisely to protect your body from side effects in the form of nausea, poisoning or indigestion. Get prior expert advice to ensure your safety.

Some essential oils have a special taste and aromatic properties, so they often find their place in the preparation of aromatic tea, sweet and meat dishes. Start adding essential oils with a small amount, literally with a couple of drops. For example, when preparing a paste, you can use rosemary oil, having previously mixed it in a tablespoon of olive. Add the resulting mixture to boiling water while cooking spaghetti, and to the finished tomato sauce you could add several drops of basil oil. For the preparation of sweet dishes, essential oils of orange, melissa, mint, lemon, lemongrass, myrrh are suitable. For drinks, for example, oils of myrrh or cinnamon are suitable. For example, instead of drinking lemon juice, you can add lemon essential oil to the water.

8. Domestic use

The properties of essential oils also help to successfully use them when cleaning the house. They prevent the propagation of bacteria, mold, fungi on various surfaces, help eliminate insects, freshen and disinfect the air indoors, fill the atmosphere at home with a pleasant aroma. But when using them, be sure to remember the occurrence of individual allergic reactions, especially in children.

- For washing: essential oils can be added to the washing machine. To do this, you can add 20-25 drops of rose oil, ylang-ylang, lemongrass, lavender or melissa to the washing powder, which pleasantly flavor bedding and towels. For example, lemon essential oil removes oil and fatty odors well.

- Natural air conditioner for laundry: Mix 0.5 liters of water in a deep container and add1 cup of 9% vinegar, 250 grams of food soda and 5 drops of geranium oil, plus drops of lavender oil. As a result, you should get an "effervescent" liquid. Pour the finished air conditioner into a clean bottle and tightly cover.

- Natural spotting agent: Apply 2-3 drops of eucalyptus oil to cotton wool or a cotton disc.

Then wipe the spot (from sweat or fat) from the edge to the center.

- Natural means for cleaning windows: Essential oils are also used for cleaning glasses. Thoroughly mix 1 cup of 9% vinegar, 1 cup of water and 10 drops of lemon oil. Pour the mixture into a spray bottle. After applying the agent to the window, wipe it with a cloth without villi.

- To wash floors: add about 35 drops of essential lemon oil in a bucket full of water, lavender or grapefruit, and you can also add a couple of drops of tea tree oil. Such a solution cleanses the floor well of various contaminants and disinfects its surface.

- Essential oils with refreshing, antimicrobial properties are suitable for washing dishes, quickly eliminating fat and microbes from surfaces. For example, several drops of essential oil of lemon, mint, tea tree, pine, eucalyptus can be mixed with the usual detergent or soda.

- For disinfection, the propagation of bacteria, mold or fungus will be eliminated. For example, an essential tea tree oil is suitable, several drops of which need to be diluted in a tablespoon of vinegar and water. The prepared solution is suitable for disinfecting kitchen shelves and crates and sponges for washing dishes.

- Essential oils with both disinfectant and bleaching properties are suitable for cleaning plumbing and tiles. These include tea tree or lemon oil, which must be mixed with water, detergent or citric acid. When applying the resulting mixture to a contaminated surface, leave the composition for a short time so that it works better, and only then rinse with water.

- Natural remedy against scale and for cleaning furniture; Mix 1 liter of vinegar, 10 drops of lemon and10 drops of sage and 10 drops of tea tree oil. Pour the finished product into a bottle and close tightly. If necessary, apply the mixture to a dirty surface or pour it onto dishes, then boil to get rid of the limescale. In addition, the agent disinfects well.

- Natural freshener for the room: Add 1 to 2 drops of your favorite oil to a spray tank filled with clean water. Spray this freshener in the rooms in the house.
Tobacco smell; oils of coniferous plants and citrus fruits are suitable.
Fragrances for dust mites: spray furniture with the addition of eucalyptus oil.

- Garbage bucket smell; It is necessary to wash the bucket well in advance. It is recommended to do this with household soap. Apply only 1 drop of essential oil of orange or tea tree to the cotton wool. Place it on the bottom of the container.

- Shoe odor; Stir 2 - 3 tablespoons food soda, 1 drop of rosemary essential oil, 1 drop of lavender oil and 1 drop of mint oil. Apply the resulting mixture to a rag and leave it in the shoes all night. A pleasant aroma will remain for the whole day.

- Vacuum cleaner dust smell; Apply 3-5 drops of essential oil of ylang-ylang or lemon to a small rag, cotton wool or cotton disc, then vacuum it with a vacuum cleaner. If there is a water tank in the vacuum cleaner, the lemon agent can be added directly there.

- Toilet odors; Synthetic air fresheners are very dangerous to human health. It is best to use natural remedies. You can also use aroma cans. A drop of any oil of a coniferous plant 1-2 times a week, will ensure the bathroom will always have a pleasant and fresh aroma.

- Refrigerator smells; Accumulate 2 - 3 drops of orange oil or lavender on a cotton disc or rag. Place it in the fridge. Essential oils remove unpleasant smells perfectly. Repeat this procedure several times for a better effect.

- To remove unpleasant odors from the surfaces of cutting boards; use essential oils of lemon, lavender, mint or tea tree, before mixing with soda. The proportion is10 drops per 100 grams of soda.

- Essential oils of citrus fruits, flowers or spices are suitable for aromatization, which will eliminate the unpleasant smell inside the cupboard or drawers of the dresser. Apply a few drops of oil to paper napkins or pieces of wood, and then spread them on the shelves.

9. Quality of essential oils

Quality essential oil in appearance transparent and homogeneous, has no precipitation. After the oil evaporates from the surface of the paper, the greasy spot must disappear. If the oil is coloured, light colouring is allowed.

Another method of determining the quality of essential oil is as follows: take 3 sheets of paper and apply one drop on the first, after 30 minutes on the second, after another 30 minutes on the third. Then smell them. The first leaf should have a weaker smell. The second is an average, more tolerant tone. The third is a fresh smell. This variety in the "tonality" of essential oils is natural, and they speak of their quality.

Of course, the property of essential oil is affected by its quality. So, it directly depends on the raw materials used to prepare the oil and on the professionalism of the person who distills the essential oil. It is worth noting that the composition and properties of essential oil can change while still in the plant. This is influenced by the time of year, the time of collection of raw materials, the climate, the type of soil, the method of cultivation and even the height of the plant above sea level.

Of course, the quality of the raw material for essential oils depends on several factors, namely:

- age of the plant, amount of precipitation, its location, the amount of sun it receives;
- at what stage of seasonal development the plant was at the time of its collection; This indicator is called biological age;
- under what conditions it was collected and processed;
- storage conditions after collection;
- plant chemotype. Simply put, the same plant produces under certain conditions in itself a different amount of some chemicals. For example, eucalyptus or thymol.
- how the plant was grown.

The method of growing the plant also affects the chemical composition of the resulting essential oil.
There are only three such methods:

1. Standard - growing plants in fields or farms.
2. Natural - growth in the wild.
3. Organic - growing under special conditions, without the use of pesticides and various chemical fertilizers.

The first problem is that often producers, in pursuit of large crops and profits, use unsafe fertilizers. Raw materials absorb all chemically harmful substances from fertilizers and thus everything ends up in squeezed oil. Such essential oil will not benefit you.

The most preferred of the above is a natural process. The plant, adapting to the environment and its conditions (sometimes very severe) and produces more useful substances.

Next is the preparation of raw materials. The quality of essential oil is influenced by the way the raw material was prepared:

- fresh - disrupted and immediately into treatment, without any preliminary preparation;
- sun drying - required if the raw material has a lot of excess moisture;
- grinding of already dried raw materials;
- Silage - grasses are collected in small stokes and kept in this form for a certain amount of time;
- soaking in water - this method is relevant for wood raw materials. Before soaking it is crushed.

Indicators of high quality of essential oil

Depending on the type of plant, the optimal method of preparing it for further conversion to essential oil is chosen. With this individual approach to raw materials, the production of the highest quality product is ensured.

Important! Each essential oil must have a quality certificate. Manufacturers undergo a very rigorous test. Transparency, appearance, color, smell of oil are evaluated. By the way, the smell should be characteristic of the name for this type of oil. No foreign impurities are allowed.

The refractive index is also estimated - the rate at which light spreads in essential oil. This speed is compared with the light propagation in the air. Further, the specific gravity and density of the oil are estimated. The rotation angle of the polarization plane is measured. This complex indicator reflects how many different components are present in the essential oil. Oil solubility in ethyl alcohol is measured. This is how the amount of hydrocarbons is checked. The proportion of non-volatile substances in oil, as well as how much moisture, ketones and aldehydes are contained in it is calculated. The acid number of the essential oil is also calculated. If all these indicators are high, the oil has been stored for a long time and has poor quality.

Chromatographic analysis is required.

Good quality essential oil should have high levels of the following:

- ✓ The proportion of esters;
- ✓ amount of esters alcohols;
- ✓ percentage of carbonyl compounds;
- ✓ amount of the main component in the essential oil.

In general, certification of essential oil is difficult, but important. As well as its subsequent selection in the store.

10. How to choose the right essential oil

Making good essential oil is a science. No less difficult to choose. Poor-quality oil extract can not only have a negative effect, but also a harmful one. The consequences of using bad oil can be headaches, fever, allergies, eczema. What do you need to focus on to avoid buying a fake or a product of poor quality?

When selecting essential oil, note the following characteristics:

✓ The quality of essential oil is a direct indicator of its healing properties. On the bottle, on the packaging, in addition to various marketing tricks, such an inscription "100% clean, natural and whole" must be indicated.
The inscriptions "100% essential oil" or "100% environmentally friendly oil" are only made by marketers.

✓ The cost of essential oil depends on the method of its extraction. Good essential oil of high quality cannot be cheap, since tens and thousands of kilograms of natural raw materials are required to produce it. High-quality raw materials, their proper preparation and processing cost a lot. From this we can conclude that the production itself is quite costly. If essential oil is cheap, then it is most likely you have its analogue, synthesized chemically version. But this does not mean that a cheaper product has no useful properties at all.

✓ The essential oil package should be made of darkened glass only for the best preservation of the oil, equipped with a dispenser and tamper protection. Otherwise, when exposed to light, the oil will oxidize and not bring proper benefits. The maximum size of the container for essential oil must be 10 ml, no more. It's all about the short shelf life.

✓ The label of the package should contain information about the raw materials - genus, type, from which part of the plant the ether is obtained (inflorescences, roots, leaves). The name of the oil should be indicated in Latin (since one botanical species of plant can have more than a hundred varieties of oil, but only a few of them are used in aromatherapy).

✓ The aroma of the present and quality essential oil cannot be sharp and concentrated, nor contain foreign impurities.

✓ Expiration date specified, country of manufacture.

✓ The package must indicate the ratio of components in the essential oil.

✓ An indicator of oil quality is the presence of eco-certificates.

Important! If when choosing oil, you found confirmation on all points, then you have a high-quality product in front of you.

Conclusion

1. Questions and answers

What essential oils are recommended for facial and body skin care?

The health and beauty of the face and body depends on the state of the skin. Wrinkles, flabby skin, exfoliation - all these factors indicate a lack of water in the body because it is 75% composed of water. To keep the skin young, tightened, fresh and elastic, it must be constantly moisturized. Rose water, based on essential rose oil, is good for this. Such water has calming properties, relieves inflammation and tones the skin, but at the same time it should not include ethyl alcohol.

Each essential oil has its own specific healing properties. In cosmetology, the properties of essential oils such as:

- ✓ stimulating,
- ✓ tonic,
- ✓ calming,
- ✓ anti-inflammatory,
- ✓ antiseptic,

   ✓ cleaning,
   ✓ moisturizing and others.

According to skin types, you can distinguish certain essential oils that will help effectively maintain beauty, according to its requests. At the same time, before use, essential oils must be combined with basic vegetable oils.

For dry skin, essential oils of lavender, geranium, neroli, roses, ylang-ylang, rosemary, jasmine, sandalwood and rose tree, majorana and dill can be used.

For oily skin, bergamot, orange, lemon, grapefruit, cypress, cedar and juniper oils are suitable, as they will help normalize the balance of the skin.

The essential oils that can be used for normal skin are: lavender, geranium, neroli, roses and lemon.

How to use essential oils properly?

Tea tree oil and lavender can be used in their pure form. All other oils need to be bred with basic cosmetic oils. Essential oils can also be added to masks, creams, scrubs, tonics and lotions.

It is recommended to use facial oils 3 times a week for general skin care. If they are used for treatment, then their use is necessary daily for 3 weeks, and after reduce the use to 3 times a week.

It is easy to prepare an oil elixir. Add 10-12 drops of essential oil to 20 ml of base oil. This amount of oil mixture is enough for a whole month. For oily skin, try light coconut oil or grape grain oil as a base. The recipe for aging skin may include, for example, lemon oils, neroli and sandalwood - it is necessary to mix 4 drops each.

Is there an effect of the skin getting used to essential oils?

From time to time, it is useful to change the formula of the oil composition, as the skin gets used to the same treatment.

What cosmetics can be made more effective with essential oils?

Essential oils are completely non-fatty - they are light,

volatile and consist of complex mixtures of organic chemicals. They quickly penetrate through all layers of the skin and enter the bloodstream. They are usually used in cosmetic oils for massage, creams and lotions, but they enter the body faster precisely when inhaled than through the skin and orally.

How to store cosmetics in which essential oils are added?

Oils can remain effective for two years with proper storage in dark glass bottles. In plastic packages, they are not recommended to be used for more than 8 weeks. It is also not worth making more than 100 ml of a mixture of body oils and 20 ml for the face. It is necessary to store oils well-closed, in a cool place. It should be remembered that without preservatives, the base will acidify the essential oil.

Can essential oils be added to the air humidifier?

Essential oils cannot be added to a conventional air humidifier, since there is a specialized oil designed for an air humidifier, or water-soluble flavors can be used. But it is worth considering that especially water-soluble flavors can cause allergies due to their chemical composition and base, so they are also undesirable to add to the humectant.

For essential oils, there are aroma diffusors (aroma lampes without candles). Accordingly, the device is electrically and itself switched off when moisture ends in it. Its main advantage is that it can mix aromatic oils in the absence of allergies.

How can essential oils be mixed together?

Essential oils can be mixed together, resulting in aromatic and therapeutic mixtures for their pleasure. When mixing aromatic oils, remember that the quality of the essential oil should be high, only in this way can they better complement each other's properties and really have a healing effect. For example:

- ✓ for the prevention of acute respiratory diseases the following can be mixed: 2 drops of tea tree oil, 2 drops of lemon, 1 drop of white thyme and 1 drop of creeping thyme;
- ✓ to improve breathing, mix essential oils - mint, eucalyptus and rosemary;

- ✓ relief from a headache - mint, lavender, lemon;
- ✓ relief from anxiety and stress - incense, bergamot, geranium;
- ✓ relief from insomnia - several drops of ylang-ylang oil and Roman chamomile;
- ✓ to cheer mood - lemongrass and rosemary.

Is the use of essential oils allowed in food?

Essential oils are widely used in food to enhance the taste of products. They are safe and are a natural flavoring for food. Citrus fruits and some floral oils are often used in sweet pastries. Sage and tarragon are added to lemonades. Mint is added to chewing gums, candy and lollipops. Also, many natural spices enhance their taste by adding essential oils to them, especially in specialized markets where they can quickly exhale.

Essential oils are usually added to enhance the smell and attract customers, for example, nutmeg, ginger oil and cloves.

Also, essential oils are often used in elite restaurants, adding to bread products. But at the same time, it is necessary to use essential oils as a food additive of high quality - they should not contain alcohol and propylene glycol in their composition, that is, natural oils without synthetic additives.

It is important to understand that this is the strongest concentrate and it cannot be overdosed otherwise will cause an allergic reaction.

Is it possible to increase immunity with essential oils?

Essential oils can increase and strengthen immunity, as they affect the central nervous system. Their use is possible as a prevention of colds, as well as during the disease. Most essential oils are excellent antiseptics and healing assistants, so they can solve several problems at once. For example:

- ✓ Eucalyptus oil is effective for lung disease from ancient times to this day, especially when inhaling or washing in a sauna. Also, coniferous essential oils are excellent for these purposes.
- ✓ Clove essential oil is widely used for lipolytics, compresses, fat-burning agents, but it cannot be used with children.
- ✓ Geranium oil will help eliminate the infection, for pain in the ear and throat, as it has warming properties. In addition, it is often added during therapeutic massage sessions, as it brings the muscles into tone.

Is the use of drugs and essential oils compatible?

The use of essential oils should not be misleading that they can be used as a conventional medicine without much analysis. With the uncontrolled prolonged use of oils, there may be negative consequences for your body, especially when people try to dissolve essential oils in water and ingest them

If allowed essential oils should ingested with food or drinks. At the same time, the joint use of essential oils with other medicines requires a mandatory preliminary consultation of a doctor.

Can essential oils be used in pregnancy?

Waiting for a child is a special time. Throughout pregnancy, a woman needs to be extremely careful about everything from food to choosing clothes. Essential oils are no exception. There are a number of strict contraindications for women in this situation.

Important note! In the first 3 months, the use of essential oils is not recommended at all. This is dangerous with a possible termination of pregnancy. Oils with ketones are extremely dangerous. In significant quantities, they are contained in tuya, basilica, wormwood, sage, rosemary of the camphor chemotype. The safest ketone is verbenone. It can be safely used to treat a dry cough, and is even suitable for young children.

These are the most important warnings.

After 12 weeks of pregnancy, oil can and even should be used. They will help to overcome depression, restore strength, tone down, calm the nervous system. Ginger will help with toxicosis. Chamomile relaxes and drives insomnia. Chamomile essential oil will heal the sore throat perfectly. Jasmine, sage and muscat are allowed to be used immediately before childbirth.

From week 18, you can use tangerine oils, neroli, preemptively spread them in almonds and wheat embryos. They are helpful in preventing stretch marks. If your legs and hands swell, you should try massages using geranium oils and basil. Pain in the lumbar will remove the mixture of lavender and rose.

Important! The oil concentration should be very small. Two drops per 10 ml of base (water, base oil or cream) are enough.

By observing these simple rules and following the recommendations, with the help of essential oils you will greatly facilitate your condition.

What essential oils are best received by children?

Essential oils, subject to precautions, can be used in the treatment of children of different ages. They can become one of the easiest ways of home health care. It is necessary to use them correctly - from dosage, ending with the appropriately chosen aromatherapy method.

At home, essential oils can be used when preparing baths, massages, aerosols or flavorers. It is recommended that children use chamomile oil, since it perfectly stimulates the strengthening of immunity and, at the same time, can be used for other unpleasant symptoms: allergies, gastrointestinal disorder, spasms and gas formation, etc.

For children's therapeutic inhalations, you can choose lavender oil or essential oils of conifers - eucalyptus or pine.

2. Result

Natural essential oils have many applications and a tremendous strength. They favorably affect the skin by moisturizing and rejuvenating. All essential oils whether they are used as a tonic or for soothing, affect the sense of smell and our nervous system. It is great that there are oils that help with diseases, affecting organs through the circulatory system.

Most modern people are deprived of the opportunity to spend every day in nature, unlike our ancestors, who spent most of their time among flowering meadows, coniferous forests, and mountain grasses.

The use of essential oils is varied, and their benefits are unusually great!

Essential oils, also called volatile oils, are natural aromatic oils, since they are granted by nature through wonderful plants.

Historically, they have been used in medicine, cosmetics, perfumes, food and aromatherapy. Essential oils are "necessary" because they contain the essence of the plant, that is, the taste or smell.

Essential oils are popular, as they have a legitimate therapeutic use based on thousands of years of experience.

 The different advantages of each particular oil with antimicrobial, anti-inflammatory properties affecting cognitive function, mood and memory, which can help weaken rigid, inflamed muscles and joints, enable a person to apply them with the best benefit for themselves.

The use of some essential oils can be applied only to the skin, others are best ingested. However, and this is important, do not take or use locally essential oils unless you are absolutely sure that they can be used in this way.

Not all essential oils are safe for ingestion, and some can irritate the skin.

Essential oils are a concentrated source of many phytochemicals, and it is recommended that essential oils be diluted with non-aromatized carrier oil for safe use on the skin.

Essential oils have firmly taken their place among other products aimed at preserving beauty.

They are a more natural, chemical-free alternative to both traditional cosmetic and potentially toxic products.

Indeed, many essential oils do not just smell pleasant, they can help solve many health problems, such as digestive problems, acne, loss of concentration and many others.

Many plants have very useful properties - they help to develop and strengthen immunity, normalize biorhythms, improve well-being, wake you up or, on the contrary, help you relax.

The range of essential oils is very wide. With their help, you can treat and prevent various diseases, care for skin and hair and also use them during love games.

The effect of the use of oils will positively affect not only your appearance, health and sexual life, but also help to solve a number of psychological problems. That is why aromatic therapy can be safely called aromatic magic.

Essential oils are often called the soul of plants. They concentrate the heat of sunlight and the cool lights of the moon.

Enjoy and be healthy using natural essential oils, and your body and soul will be in harmony with nature!

Stay healthy and enjoy the benefits of a long, full life!

I really hope you enjoyed this book and found the information useful. You may also want to read two more books about health and well-being:

1. Peptides: The Secret of Health and Longevity. The Formula for a Youthful Life. How Vitamins and Minerals Can Improve Your Life's Quality. You can get it here https://www.amazon.com/dp/B089WJCDT6

2. Peptides in Cosmetology: The Anti-Aging Power of Peptides in Cosmetics for Skin Rejuvenation. How Peptides Can Improve Overall Health and Wellbeing. You can get it here https://www.amazon.com/dp/B08FBKQSJY

Both books will help you learn about the modern possibilities of peptides and the power they have to heal and rejuvenate the human body.

Leave Your Review

As an independent author with a small marketing budget, I live for reviews on this platform. I love hearing from my readers and I personally read every single review.
If you enjoyed this book, let me know by leaving honest feedback.
You can do that by simply clicking the link below.
Looking forward to your feedback!

Leave your review here by typing in the search bar
https://www.amazon.com/dp/B08HZ2GS4C